Pandas

by Kimberlee Mason

MODERN CURRICULUM PRESS
Pearson Learning Group

My name is Su-Lin.
I live in China.

Pandas live in China too.
I like pandas.

Pandas are big animals.
Their fur is black and white.

What do pandas do?
Watch!
See their habits.

Pandas climb.

Pandas hide.

Pandas swim.

Pandas slide.

Pandas sit.

Pandas play.

Pandas eat—night and day!

Pandas are big animals.

Pandas roll.

Pandas creep.

Shhh! Pandas also like to sleep!